The Buffalo Soldiers

by Alice K. Flanagan

Content Adviser: Lynda Morgan,
Associate Professor of History, Chair of the History Department,
Mount Holyoke College, Massachusetts

Reading Adviser: Susan Kesselring, M.A.,
Literacy Educator,
Rosemount-Apple Valley-Eagan (Minnesota) School District

COMPASS POINT BOOKS
MINNEAPOLIS, MINNESOTA

Compass Point Books
3109 West 50th Street, #115
Minneapolis, MN 55410

Visit Compass Point Books on the Internet at *www.compasspointbooks.com*
or e-mail your request to *custserv@compasspointbooks.com*

On the cover: Buffalo Soldiers of the 25th Infantry Regiment at Fort Keogh, Montana, in 1890

Photographs ©: Library of Congress, cover, back cover, 5, 10, 13, 16, 30, 33, 36, 41; Prints Old and Rare, back cover (far left); North Wind Picture Archives, 4, 8, 23, 27; Courtesy Don Stivers, 6, 29; American Stock/Getty Images, 7; The Denver Public Library, Western History Department, call number X-31308, 11; Bettmann/Corbis, 12; The Denver Public Library, Western History Department, call number X-32022, 15; Nebraska State Historical Society, 19; Art courtesy Burl Washington, photo by Lee Angle Photography, 20; Robert Holmes/Corbis, 21; John Elk III, 22; DVIC/NARA, 24, 38; *Ambush at the Ancient Rocks* by Frank C. McCarthy, The Greenwich Workshop, Inc., 25; The Denver Public Library, Western History Department, call number X-32141, 26; Courtesy of the Arizona Historical Society/Tucson, AHS#19705, 28; DigitalVision, 31; Minnesota Historical Society, 34; U.S. Army Photo, sculptor Eddie Dixon, 39; Arnold Sachs/Consolidated News Pictures/Getty Images, 40.

Creative Director: Terri Foley
Managing Editor: Catherine Neitge
Editor: Nadia Higgins
Photo Researcher: Svetlana Zhurkina
Designer/Page production: Bradfordesign, Inc./Bobbie Nuytten
Cartographer: XNR Productions, Inc.
Educational Consultant: Diane Smolinski

Library of Congress Cataloging-in-Publication Data
Flanagan, Alice K.
  The Buffalo Soldiers / by Alice K. Flanagan.
    p. cm.—(We the people)
  Includes bibliographical references and index.
  ISBN 0-7565-0833-9 (hardcover)
African Americans—West (U.S.)—History—19th century—Juvenile literature. 2. African American soldiers—West (U.S.)—History—19th century—Juvenile literature. 3. United States. Army—African American troops—History—19th century—Juvenile literature. 4. Frontier and pioneer life—West (U.S.)—Juvenile literature. 5. Indians of North America—Wars—1866-1895—Juvenile literature. 6. West (U.S.)—History—Juvenile literature. 7. United States. Army. Cavalry, 9th—Juvenile literature. 8. United States. Army. Cavalry, 10th—Juvenile literature.
I. Title. II. We the people (Series) (Compass Point Books)
  E185.925.F58 2005
  973.7'415—dc22   2004016205

TABLE OF CONTENTS

SOLDIERS ON PATROL

A covered wagon slowly made its way along a dusty dirt road in Arizona. The year was 1889. A small group of U.S. soldiers riding alongside the wagon guarded the more than $28,000 that was hidden within it. The money, which was going to be used to pay Army soldiers' salaries, was a large amount for those days. As they made their way, the guards constantly kept watch for thieves eager to get their hands on all that cash.

Buffalo Soldiers traveling through the Arizona desert

Isaiah Mays, around 1900, wearing his Medal of Honor

Along the route, they came upon a huge boulder blocking the road. The soldiers stopped to push it aside. It was a trap! Suddenly, bandits began shooting at the soldiers. The gunfire continued for more than a half-hour. When most of the soldiers were badly wounded, the thieves made off with the Army payroll.

Two soldiers, Benjamin Brown and Isaiah Mays, had been shot while removing the boulder from the road. Yet Brown continued to fight, and Mays ran miles to get help. For their bravery, each man later received a Medal of Honor, the nation's highest military award.

These two soldiers and the rest of their troop were an extraordinary sight on the American frontier in 1889. They were black men serving their country in special all-black units of the U.S. Army. Called Buffalo Soldiers, these units were the first of their kind in the Army's history. They would play an important role on the Western Frontier.

A Buffalo Soldier serving on the Western Frontier in the late 1800s

NEW ALL-BLACK UNITS

In 1866, the territory known as the Western Frontier of the United States was a very violent place. Bandits and cattle thieves were roaming freely on the open plains. American Indians were fighting settlers who were taking their land. In an effort to keep law and order, the U.S. government began to build more forts on the Western Frontier and sent troops to guard them.

Masked gunmen cut wire fences in order to steal cattle from a ranch in Nebraska around 1885.

7

Plains Indians attack a wagon train of settlers in the 1800s.

Forts made settlers and travelers feel secure and provided
safe places to go to for help on the vast frontier. The troops protected people from bandits and Indians at war. Eventually, roads,
schools, churches, and entire towns sprang up around the forts.

8

A map of the Western Frontier in the late 1800s, showing important forts where the Buffalo Soldiers served

Among the troops were black soldiers who would come to be known as Buffalo Soldiers. In those days, the military was segregated, which means that black and white soldiers were not allowed to serve in the same units.

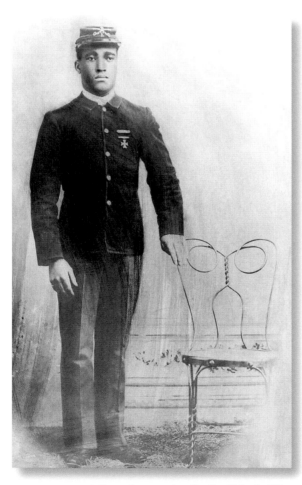

A formal portrait of a Buffalo Soldier from the 9th Cavalry Regiment

Buffalo Soldiers had six of their own regiments, or military units, which had been specially created by Congress in 1866. In 1869, the six regiments were reduced to four: the 9th and 10th Cavalry Regiments (for horse-men) and the 24th and 25th Infantry Regiments (for soldiers on foot).

10

Each of these regiments consisted of around 1,000 men, commanded by white officers. By the late 1800s, the Buffalo Soldiers would have black officers. Men such as Henry O. Flipper graduated from the U.S.

A cavalry soldier on the Pine Ridge Indian Reservation, South Dakota, in 1891

Military Academy at West Point and earned the title of officer. However, he and other outstanding black officers were never allowed to command regiments.

The Buffalo Soldiers were not the first black men to serve in the U.S.

Henry O. Flipper as a cadet at the U.S. Military Academy at West Point in New York

military. More than 200,000 African-Americans had fought in the Civil War (1861–1865). As members of the four new regiments, however, Buffalo Soldiers would be part of the regular Army. They would

12

receive a steady salary and live in Army housing, even
though it was separate from the white soldiers and not
in the best condition.

Buffalo Soldiers of the 25th Infantry Regiment in 1890

Not everyone had been in favor of adding African-American regiments to the regular Army. Many congressmen believed that white soldiers performed better than black soldiers. However, others thought that African-Americans had served well in the Civil War and should be given an opportunity to advance within the ranks of the Army.

During the Civil War, around 40,000 African-American troops had lost their lives. Twenty-three black soldiers had been given the Medal of Honor. Based on these outstanding service records, Congress voted to include all-black regiments in the regular Army. Eventually, the soldiers in these regiments were nicknamed Buffalo Soldiers.

CALL THEM "BUFFALO SOLDIERS"

Reports vary on how the Buffalo Soldiers got their nickname. It is generally believed that the 10th Cavalry first used it in the 1870s. Later, all African-American soldiers who served in all-black units of the U.S. Army were called Buffalo Soldiers.

Some say the Cheyenne Indians named the 10th Cavalry Buffalo Soldiers in 1867, following a fierce

Cheyenne Indians in the late 1800s

15

two-day battle near Fort Leavenworth, Kansas. During the fight, 90 cavalrymen held off 800 Cheyenne warriors, losing only three men. When the Indian warriors saw how hard the black soldiers had fought, they compared them to buffalo. Buffalo act fiercely when cornered or wounded and are greatly respected by Indians.

Buffalo-fur robes such as this one may have prompted the nickname Buffalo Soldier.

Other historians say the name was given to the soldiers because their dark woolly hair looked like buffalo hair. The name also might have come from the way the soldiers looked when they wore heavy buffalo robes in winter. Regardless of when or where the soldiers were nicknamed, the men took it as a sign of respect from the Indians. Eventually, the 10th Cavalry even added an image of the buffalo to the design of its flag.

WHY THEY JOINED THE ARMY

With the creation of the four all-black units, many young African-Americans joined the Army for three- or five-year assignments. Between 1866 and 1867, almost 2,000 men joined the 9th and 10th Cavalry Regiments and were sent out West. Most of them had come from Southern states, such as Louisiana and Kentucky. Others had come from Northern states such as New York and Connecticut.

They joined the Army to better their lives. One young man gave up farming to become a soldier. As he put it, "I got tired of looking mules in the face from sunrise to sunset. [I] thought there must be a better livin' in this world."

For these men, a better living included getting paid regularly. A steady paycheck of $13 a month looked good to those who might never earn as much working other jobs. Besides steady pay, military service promised housing, education, medical attention, and even a pension that would be paid to them after they retired. All of these benefits sounded attractive to the African-Americans, who dreamed of saving up enough money to own land and build homes of their own someday.

Others joined in hopes of escaping the unfair treatment they faced at home and finding freedom out West. The Civil War had brought an end to slavery in the United States. While this was a major improvement in their lives, African-Americans were still being denied many of the opportunities and freedoms that white people had. As soldiers, these African-Americans hoped to gain the respect they had never experienced as slaves. Unfortunately, disrespect and discrimination followed them into the Army.

The first Buffalo Soldiers came from different walks of life. There were men who had fought in the Civil War, such as Jacob Wilks and George Washington Williams. Others who joined had no military experience at all.

George Jordan was a former slave from Tennessee who went on to earn a Medal of Honor for bravery in combat. Cathay Williams, a young woman from Missouri, disguised herself as a man in order to serve as a cook in the Army. She joined the infantry as

Sergeant George Jordan (third from left, bottom row, wearing a hat with a full brim) served in the 9th Cavalry's K troop.

Cathay Williams disguised herself as a man in order to join the Army.

William Cathay. When asked why she joined, she said, "I wanted to make my own living and not be dependent on relatives or friends."

The ages of those who joined ranged from 18 to 34. However, 20- and 21-year-olds were the largest group. Many had been slaves. Most had little or no education, no military experience, and no idea how to survive on the dangerous Western Frontier. As one new soldier wrote, they were "clothed, armed, drilled, mounted, and sent out on the Plains as fast as they arrived."

DAILY LIFE

Frontier life was difficult. Temperatures ranged from very hot to extremely cold. Wild animals, such as mountain lions and wolves, could attack at any time. Without maps to guide the soldiers as they patrolled the remote mountain and desert areas, they risked getting lost and dying. Many of the forts they were sent to were not fit to live in. The soldiers were packed into filthy shacks called barracks. Many became sick with colds, diarrhea, and a deadly illness of the lungs called tuberculosis.

An actor dressed as a Buffalo Soldier re-creates life at camp on the Western Frontier.

21

Generally, African-American troops served the longest periods in the most remote posts in the Southwest. Their horses and equipment were not as good as what the white soldiers were given. The food given to them was poor. A surgeon at a fort in New Mexico claimed that black soldiers "had none of the staples common at other posts. The butter was made of

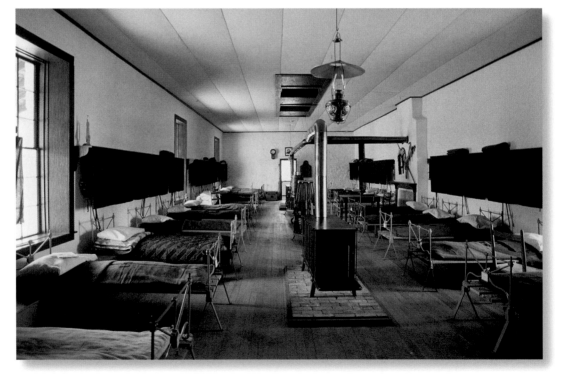

Soldiers slept in cramped barracks such as this at Fort Davis, Texas.

suet [animal fat (instead of cream)] and there was only enough flour for the officers [not for regular soldiers]."

The way black soldiers were treated in frontier towns wasn't any better. Even though they made the towns safer, they were often called names and attacked by people who did not respect them. These people hated the sight of black men wearing U.S. Army uniforms.

A frontier town from the late 1800s

THE 10TH CAVALRY

The 10th Cavalry headed for the Western Frontier in the summer and fall of 1867. Its orders were to maintain law and order between settlers and Indian tribes. Colonel Benjamin Grierson, a white man, would lead the regiment for the next 22 years.

During those 22 years of service, the 10th Cavalry lived at many forts throughout Kansas, Texas, and Indian

Members of the 10th Cavalry around 1898

Cavalry members patrolled dangerous areas.

Territory (Oklahoma). Some of its duties included stringing miles of new telegraph wire, protecting workers who were building railroads, and tracking down hunters who were illegally killing buffalo on Indian lands.

The 10th Cavalry also patrolled the borders of the Indian reservations. Reservations were specific areas of land that the U.S. government forced the Indians to live on. These areas were meant to keep Indians apart from settlers.

So, as part of their duties, the soldiers kept Indians from leaving their reservations. However, the soldiers rarely kept settlers out.

Because Indians were not allowed to leave the reservations—even to hunt—the U.S. government promised to provide them with food and supplies. However, the government failed to give them these things, and the Indians became desperate to find food. Many were forced to raid towns and ranches to get what they needed to survive. Then the Buffalo Soldiers were ordered to bring them back.

The Kiowa-Comanche reservation, Indian Territory (Oklahoma), in the late 1800s

To control the Indians more closely, the U.S. government built forts on the reservations. The Buffalo Soldiers built Fort Sill in the center of the Kiowa-Comanche reservation in what is now Oklahoma. It served as the government agency for several tribes. Indians often went there to trade goods and get help with their problems.

In 1873, the 10th moved from Fort Sill to forts in Texas. That summer about 400 soldiers from the 10th Cavalry and the 24th and 25th Infantry Regiments went to explore an unmapped region of northwestern Texas and northeastern New Mexico known as the Staked Plains, or Llano Estacado (pronounced YAH-no es-tah-KAH-doe). Dressed in the Army's

A soldier falls off his horse while making his way through difficult terrain.

27

heavy, wool uniforms and battling temperatures of more than 100 degrees Fahrenheit (38 degrees Celsius), the soldiers traveled for six months through the dry, treeless area. They made maps of the region, marking every source of water they found. After covering almost 10,000 miles (16,000 kilometers), the soldiers returned with information that would help future settlers know the best locations to build towns.

Another of the unit's important duties was to help track down the Apache Indian leader Victorio and his followers. Victorio had agreed to live on a reservation. However, when his people began starving, he left the reservation to hunt and raid ranches

Apache leader Victorio

28

throughout Mexico, Texas, and New Mexico. Victorio started attacking settlers when they began building homes on reservation land and stealing Apache horses. The 10th Cavalry tracked Victorio but never captured him. Eventually, Mexican soldiers killed Victorio and many of his followers in Mexico.

Members of the 10th Cavalry in search of Apache leader Victorio

THE 9TH CAVALRY

The men of the 9th U.S. Cavalry Regiment left for the Western Frontier about the same time as the men of the 10th began arriving at their posts in 1867. The 9th made its quarters at Fort Stockton and Fort Davis in West Texas. Colonel Edward Hatch was the regiment's white commander and would lead them for 23 years.

One of this cavalry's main duties included patrolling the Texas territory, which was a particularly difficult task. The area included thousands of square miles of thick shrubs and trees along the Rio Grande (the river that forms a border with Mexico), huge desert regions, and

Members of the 9th Cavalry Regiment around 1898

Rugged land along the Rio Grande provided many obstacles to cavalrymen on patrol.

rugged mountains. Frequent Indian attacks were making life very dangerous for settlers. Mexican bandits and American outlaws were robbing stagecoaches that carried mail and other important items across the territory. The 9th worked to protect the stagecoach routes, control the Indians, and maintain general law and order in the midst of these dangerous conditions.

In 1875, the 9th Cavalry was moved to New Mexico to track down Apaches found off their reservations. Ten years later, soldiers were tracking down and removing settlers who were illegally occupying land on the Apache reservation. In 1885,

31

men of the 9th were transferred to forts in Nebraska to patrol the reservations of the Lakota Sioux Indians. When U.S. Army troops massacred 350 Lakota Indians at Wounded Knee Creek in South Dakota in 1890, the men of the 9th were ordered to care for the wounded Indians and bury the dead.

For more than 20 years, the 9th and 10th Cavalry Regiments served on the frontier from Montana to Texas, along the Rio Grande into New Mexico, in Arizona, Colorado, and the Dakotas, and along the U.S.-Mexico border. They served in small, scattered units as they patrolled the huge territory assigned to them. Following military orders, they had built forts, protected settlers, and mapped new territories. Among their most difficult duties, however, was forcing Indians from their homelands and onto reservations. Although this opened the West to future settlement, it did so by denying freedom and opportunity to many people.

HARPER'S WEEKLY.

JOURNAL OF CIVILIZATION.

VOL. XXX.—No. 1548.
Copyright, 1886, by Harper & Brothers.

NEW YORK, SATURDAY, AUGUST 21, 1886.

TEN CENTS A COPY.
WITH A SUPPLEMENT.

A wounded Buffalo Soldier is rescued during an attack.

33

THE INFANTRY REGIMENTS

Generally, infantry regiments (those on foot) worked within and around the forts. For almost 30 years, units of the 24th and 25th Infantry Regiments built and repaired forts, constructed roads, put up telegraph lines, and guarded sources of water from

Company I of the 25th Infantry Regiment in 1883

enemies who might damage them. Some of their other duties included building and operating a lumber camp and sawmill, guarding food and supply routes, and carrying out scouting parties to protect travelers and stagecoaches from attacks by Indians and Mexican bandits.

Along with troops of the 9th and 10th Cavalry Regiments, Company H of the 24th Infantry chased the Apache leader Victorio in 1880. Colonel Hatch, commander of the 9th Cavalry, described the search for Victorio in a letter to a general. "The work performed by these troops is most arduous [difficult]," he wrote. "The horses [are] worn to mere shadows. [The] men [are] nearly without boots, shoes and clothing." Hatch went on to say that the men traveled on rough mountain trails for days without food and water. In the end, they returned without finding Victorio.

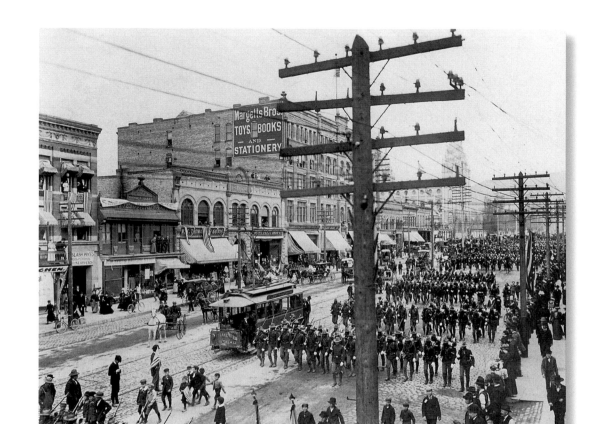

Members of the 24th Infantry Regiment march down a
street in Salt Lake City, Utah, in 1898.

Without the work of the 24th and 25th
Infantry and the 9th and 10th Cavalry Regiments,
the rapid growth of the Western Frontier might
never have been possible.

WHY WE HONOR THEM

By the end of the 1890s, many of the original Buffalo Soldiers had died or retired. Some of those who retired had taken up farming in the West. Others became leaders in their communities. Several were hired as cowboys on ranches throughout the West.

During their service, these Buffalo Soldiers had helped build the West. They paved the way for eight new states to become part of the Union: Colorado, North Dakota, South Dakota, Montana, Utah, Oklahoma, New Mexico, and Arizona.

In 1898, all four black regiments were sent to Cuba to fight in the Spanish-American War. They also served proudly in the Philippines. From 1903 to 1916, the 9th and 10th Cavalry Regiments served at home, patrolling the national parks in California.

When the United States sent troops into battle during the First and Second World Wars and the Korean War, Buffalo Soldiers served once again. In 1953, the U.S. Army

Buffalo Soldiers during World War II (1941–1945)

integrated its fighting units. From then on, units were made up of soldiers of all races, fighting side by side.

Eventually, the history of the Buffalo Soldiers was forgotten—but not by members of the 9th and 10th Cavalry. They created an organization to remember the history of their former units. The 9th and 10th (Horse) Cavalry Association still exists today.

Now a monument stands at Fort Leavenworth, Kansas, to honor the Buffalo Soldiers for their service to their country. The bronze sculpture is the result of the

The Buffalo Soldier Monument at Fort Leavenworth, Kansas

efforts of General Colin Powell. Powell was the first

black chairman of the Joint Chiefs of Staff, which is

the highest group in the U.S. military. Powell's speech

at the dedication of the monument on July 25, 1992,

praised the Buffalo Soldier.

He said, "Look at him, Soldier of the Nation—courageous, iron-willed, every bit the soldier that his white brother was." Then he said that even though "African-Americans had answered the country's every call," they had never received "the fame and fortune" that they deserved. Yet

General Colin Powell

they fought for a better future for themselves and others. "The Buffalo Soldier," said Powell, "believed that hatred and bigotry and prejudice could not defeat him, that ... someday, through his efforts and the efforts of others to follow, future generations would know full freedom."

Like the black soldiers who had fought in the Civil War to end slavery, the Buffalo Soldiers also fought for freedom. Though they were not slaves, they still could not live or work or move about as they wanted in society. By serving as soldiers in the Army, they believed they would earn the respect of those who were denying them their freedom. Once they had gained this respect, they thought their lives would be better. They fought for freedom not only for themselves but for future generations as well.

In 1912, Buffalo Soldier veterans marched in a parade in New York City. Today, Buffalo Soldiers are widely honored for their courage in the face of racism and hardship.

41

GLOSSARY

barracks—buildings for soldiers to live in

bigotry—refusing to respect someone else's point of view, especially in matters of race

cavalry—soldiers who ride horses

discrimination—treating people unfairly because of their race, religion, sex, or age

infantry—soldiers who fight on foot

integrated—made up of people of all races who have been brought together

pension—money paid regularly to people who have retired from work

plains—broad, flat land

segregated—separated by race

stagecoach—a coach drawn by horses that carries mail, passengers, and baggage

DID YOU KNOW?

- The motto of the 9th Cavalry was "We can, we will." The motto of the 10th Cavalry was "Ready and forward."

- In the 1880s, white regiments of the U.S. Army were given flags to identify their units. African-American regiments had to make their own.

- A chaplain was assigned to each black regiment to provide spiritual guidance and to teach the soldiers reading, writing, and math. In 1884, Henry V. Plummer became the first African-American to serve as chaplain. He was assigned to the 9th Cavalry at Fort Riley, Kansas.

- Soldiers from the 9th Cavalry served as the Honor Guard for President Theodore Roosevelt when he visited San Francisco in 1903. This was the first time black soldiers had served as an escort for a president of the United States.

- Sergeant George Jordan, a Buffalo Soldier who received a Medal of Honor in 1890, was honored once again more than 100 years later. In 1999, the Army's 6th Recruiting Brigade dedicated its headquarters for the Western region to George Jordan. The headquarters are located on Sergeant Jordan Avenue in North Las Vegas, Nevada.

IMPORTANT DATES

Timeline

1866	Congress approves the enlistment of African-American soldiers in the regular Army, resulting in the formation of the 9th and 10th Cavalry and the 24th and 25th Infantry Regiments.
1867	African-American regiments are sent to the Western Frontier.
1877	Lieutenant Henry O. Flipper becomes the first African-American to graduate from West Point and the first African-American officer in any of the Buffalo Soldier regiments.
1953	All fighting units in the American Armed Forces are integrated.
1992	The Buffalo Soldier Monument is unveiled at Fort Leavenworth, Kansas.

IMPORTANT PEOPLE

HENRY O. FLIPPER (1856-1940)
First African-American to graduate from the U.S. Military Academy at West Point and serve as an officer in the 10th Cavalry

COLONEL BENJAMIN H. GRIERSON (1826-1911)
Commander of the 10th Cavalry for 22 years

COLONEL EDWARD HATCH (1832-1889)
Commander of the 9th Cavalry for 23 years and a Civil War hero

GENERAL COLIN L. POWELL (1937-)
First African-American four-star general of the United States and chairman of the Joint Chiefs of Staff; through his efforts, a memorial to the Buffalo Soldiers was built at Fort Leavenworth, Kansas

WANT TO KNOW MORE?

At the Library

Barnett, Tracy. *The Buffalo Soldiers.* Broomall, Pa.: Mason Crest, 2003.

Bolden, Tonya, and Gail Buckley. *American Patriots: The Story of Blacks in the Military from the Revolution to Desert Storm.* New York: Crown Publishers, 2003.

Finlayson, Reggie. *Colin Powell.* Minneapolis: Lerner Publications, 2004.

Hooker, Forrestine C. *Child of the Fighting Tenth: On the Frontier with the Buffalo Soldiers.* New York: Oxford University Press, 2003.

On the Web

For more information on the *Buffalo Soldiers,* use FactHound to track down Web sites related to this book.

1. Go to *www.facthound.com*

2. Type in a search word related to this book or this book ID: 0756508339.

3. Click on the *Fetch It* button.

Your trusty FactHound will fetch the best Web sites for you!

On the Road

The Buffalo Soldiers National Museum
1834 Southmore
Houston, TX 77004
713/942-8920
To see photos and other military memorabilia of the Buffalo Soldiers

Fort Sill National Historic Landmark & Museum
437 Quanah Road
Fort Sill, OK 73503-5100
To see cavalry barracks, a guardhouse, warehouses built by the 9th and 10th Cavalry units in the 1870s.

Look for more We the People books about this era:

The Alamo

The Arapaho and Their History

The Battle of the Little Bighorn

The California Gold Rush

The Chumash and Their History

The Creek and Their History

The Erie Canal

Great Women of the Old West

The Lewis and Clark Expedition

The Louisiana Purchase

The Mexican War

The Ojibwe and Their History

The Oregon Trail

The Pony Express

The Santa Fe Trail

The Trail of Tears

The Transcontinental Railroad

The Wampanoag and Their History

The War of 1812

A complete list of We the People titles is available on our Web site:
www.compasspointbooks.com

INDEX

About the Author

Alice K. Flanagan writes books for children and teachers. Since she was a young girl, she has enjoyed writing. She has written more than 70 books. Some of her books include biographies of U.S. presidents and their wives, biographies of people working in our neighborhoods, phonics books for beginning readers, and informational books about birds and Native Americans. Alice K. Flanagan lives in Chicago.